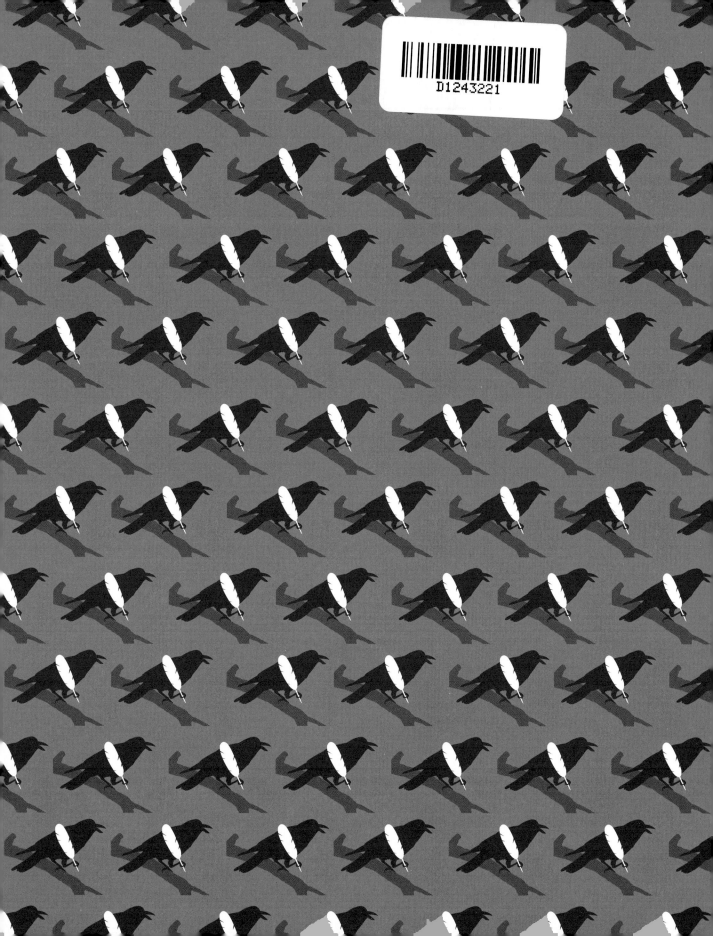

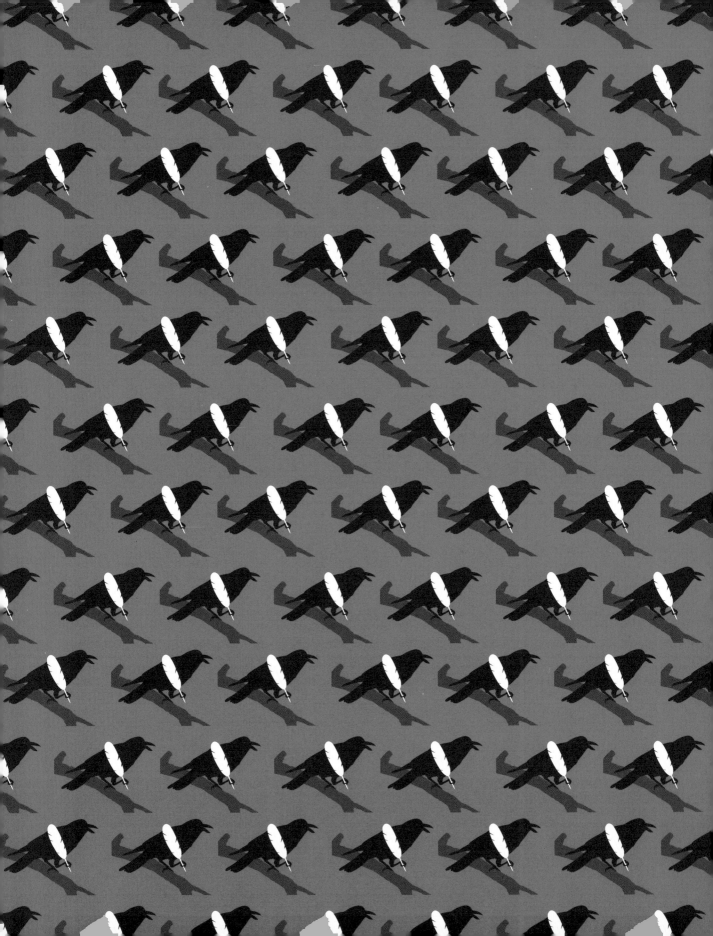

SHAKESPEARE

GREAT LIVES IN GRAPHICS

Button
BOOKS

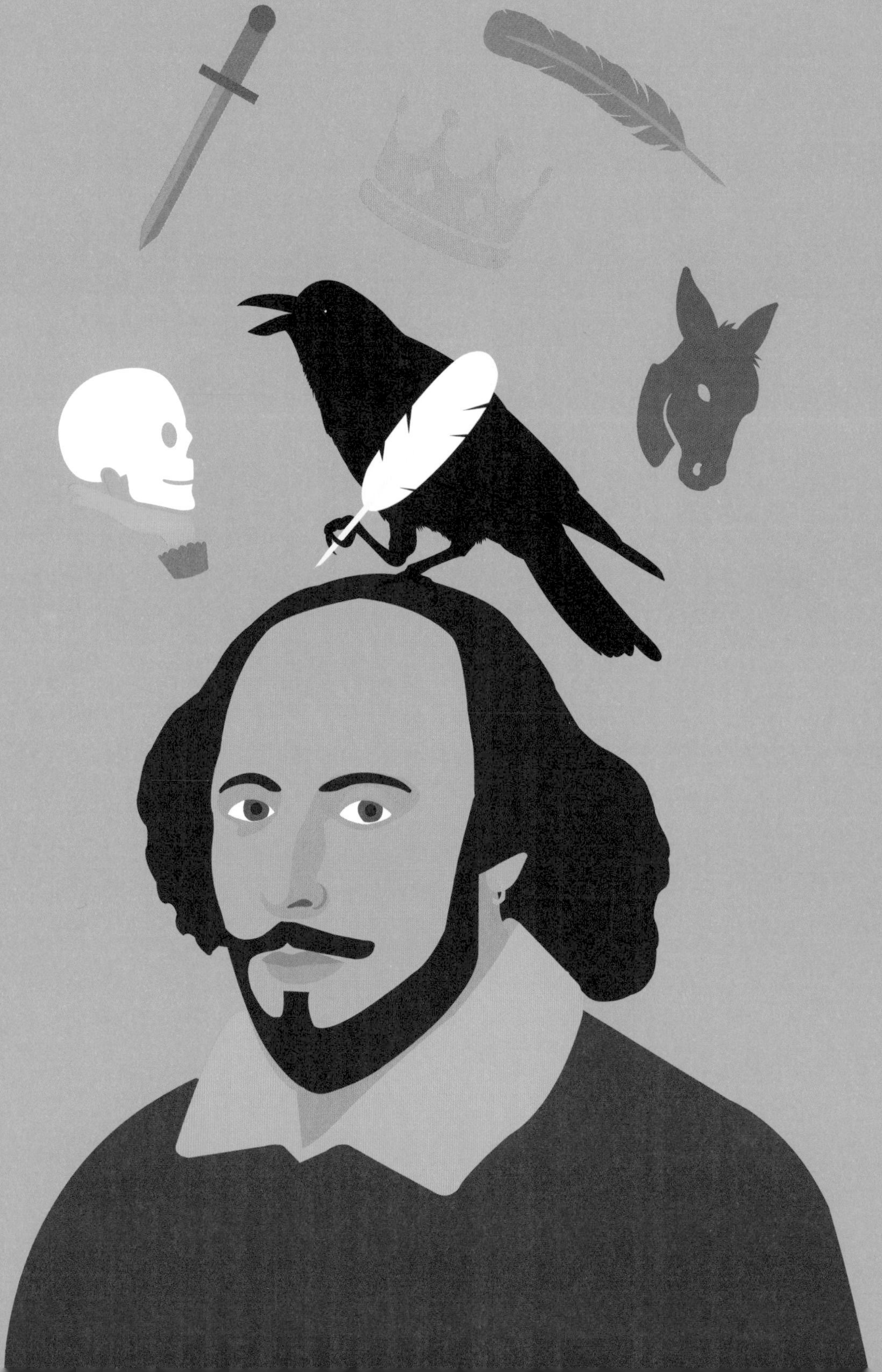

At first glance, **William Shakespeare's** early life may not seem that exciting. He grew up in a small town in Tudor England, where he probably spent most of his time at school or playing in the nearby fields. But in many ways this makes his story more interesting. How did a country boy with no university education go on to write some of the most amazing plays of all time?

The answer is simple. Will's works are special because they're about life and what it's like to be a person, something no university course could have taught him. He had a gift for understanding the way that people think and feel and for expressing those emotions on paper. Love, death, jealousy, fear, rage, hope, laughter, and revenge–his plays take all of what it means to be human and weave it into wonderful stories, sprinkled with clever word play. And it's important to remember that Will wrote them to be performed on stage in front of an audience. His dramas had to please the young, old, rich, and poor alike, or he would have been out of a job. Will wasn't trying to write great literature. He wanted people (like you!) to enjoy watching them. As Hamlet said, "The play's the thing!"

Will's WORLD

1588 English Navy defeats the Spanish Armada

1587 Mary, Queen of Scots, is executed at the Tower of London

1592 Will moves to London and starts writing plays

1564 Will is born in April in Stratford-upon-Avon, England

1571 Will probably starts school around this time

1585 Will's twins, Judith and Hamnet, are born

1593 Plague closes the theaters, so Will writes poems instead

1580 Francis Drake returns to England in the *Golden Hind*

1584 Queen gives Sir Walter Raleigh permission to explore New World

1594 Will joins an acting company

1582 Will marries Anne Hathaway

1583 Will's daughter Susanna is born

1596 Will's son Hamnet dies aged 11

R.I.P. HAMNET

1597
Will buys a swanky new house in Stratford

1610
Galileo sees Jupiter's moons through his telescope

1609
Will's sonnets are published

1611
King James Bible is published in English

1598
Will's plays, including *Romeo & Juliet* and *A Midsummer Night's Dream*, are popular

1605
The Gunpowder Plot

1612
Will moves to Stratford

1599
The Globe theater is built in London

1613
The Globe burns down and is rebuilt

1603
Queen Elizabeth I dies, James I is King of England

1616
Will dies on April 23, thought to be his 52nd birthday

R.I.P.
APRIL 23
1616
(Age 52)

R.I.P.
DAD

1601
Will's dad dies and he starts writing tragedies, such as *Hamlet* and *Macbeth*

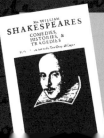

1623
His plays are published as the First Folio

COUNTRY BOY

Will grew up surrounded by the English countryside and spent most of his time either at school or playing in the woods and fields near his home. Here's what rural life was like at the time . . .

· HANDY MAN ·

Will's dad was a glover who sold his goods from a window at one end of the house to customers in the street outside. He turned animal skins into leather in his back garden using a process called tanning, which involved soaking the skins in pits of urine to soften them!

POOR PEOPLE sold their **URINE** to tanners, so one of young Will's first chores may have been to help his dad collect it from them. Yuk!

TUDOR GENTS usually carried at least seven pairs of gloves and used different ones for eating, drinking, and even sleeping.

7x 🧤🧤🧤 🧤🧤🧤

QUEEN ELIZABETH I was a glove fan. Legend has it she owned more than:

x2000

70+
references to gloves and glove-making in Will's plays.

WHERE DID WILL LIVE?

Born in the small town of STRATFORD-UPON-AVON, Will grew up in a crowded thatched cottage with his three younger brothers and two little sisters. His mom Mary was a farmer's daughter, while his dad John made gloves and became a town leader.

SMALL WONDER

Stratford only had eight or nine streets when Will lived there.

1564
1,500 people

TODAY
30,000+ people

WHAT WAS COUNTRY LIFE LIKE?

Farming was hard work and people depended on their crops to survive.

HOW WERE ANIMALS USED?

GOATS
Used for milk, horn, leather, and meat.

SHEEP
Used for wool, milk, leather, and meat.

COWS
Mostly used to pull plows.

WHAT DID COUNTRY FOLK **DO FOR FUN?**

With no phones, TV, or even electricity, people had to make their own entertainment.

TUDORS ALSO ENJOYED:

 BOARD GAMES

 HAWKING

 DICE

 **ARCHERY**

 COCK FIGHTS

SOCCER

Two enormous teams would try to pass a ball through markers at each end of town by any means necessary. Unsurprisingly, games often ended with broken bones!

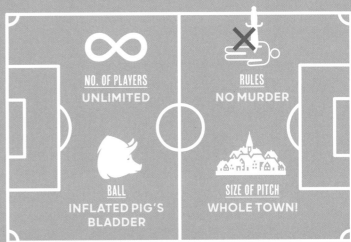

∞
NO. OF PLAYERS
UNLIMITED

✗
RULES
NO MURDER

BALL
INFLATED PIG'S BLADDER

SIZE OF PITCH
WHOLE TOWN!

---

5 A.M.–7 P.M.

Average working day:
REST
WORK

90%
of people lived in the countryside in Tudor England.

PLANTS & POTIONS

Young Will knew which flowers and herbs worked well in cooking and medicine and used his knowledge to add interest to his plays.

ROMEO & JULIET Juliet drinks a sleeping draft made from deadly nightshade.

MACBETH The witches use root of hemlock in their potion.

A MIDSUMMER NIGHT'S DREAM Mischievous fairy Puck makes a love potion from a flower called "love-in-idleness."

PIGS

When a pig was killed, nothing was wasted. Even its bristles were used to make brushes!

MINI MUTTON

Sheep were smaller in Tudor times, more like a medium-sized, woolly dog.

1600 — **46** LBS

TODAY — **120** LBS

STORY CORNER

Young Will was lucky to be part of a great storytelling culture. In the evenings families gathered around their fire at home to tell folk tales and medieval stories about legends such as King Arthur and Robin Hood.

SCHOOL RULES

School was tough in Tudor times. Poor Will learned nothing but Latin. No art, no history, no science. Just Latin grammar, from dawn to dusk. No wonder he left school at 14!

LITTLE LEARNERS

When he was four, it's likely Will went to a petty school (a small private school run by a local housewife at her home) where he would have learned to:

 Get up early

Say his prayers

Respect mom and dad

Eat nicely

 Read English

Tudor children learned their letters from a hornbook– a wooden frame with a page showing the alphabet and Lord's Prayer, protected by a sheet of transparent horn.

I L~~OVE~~ HATE ← SCHOOL

 NO sports

Same lesson all day, every day: **LATIN**

NO vacations

Must speak Latin AT ALL T...

EXAMS every Friday

Hours: 6A.M.–

NO girls allowed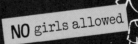

SIX DAYS

At seven, Will probably joined the local grammar school. Most boys didn't like it–I wonder why?

BEHAVE, OR ELSE!

Tudor teachers were very strict. Caught speaking English in the corridors? That'll be 50 strokes of the cane! Pupils with rich families sometimes paid for a "whipping-boy" for their child. If the wealthy child misbehaved, the whipping-boy was caned instead!

OUCH!

50x

DID YOU KNOW?

In just seven years, Will would have spent **2,000 HOURS** at school! That's TWICE the number of hours kids spend at school today.

One of young Will's favorite writers was the Roman poet OVID, whose poem *Metamorphoses* is a collection of stories taken from Greek and Roman myths.

FAVORITE WRITER →

MIND YOUR LANGUAGE!

When Will was young, Latin was the language of educated Europe and if you wanted a good job you had to speak it fluently, which wasn't easy! Here's how long it takes most English speakers to learn other languages around the world...

EASY

TIME TO LEARN
6 MONTHS/600 HOURS

SPANISH	460 million speakers
PORTUGUESE	220 million speakers
FRENCH	77 million speakers
ITALIAN	65 million speakers

MEDIUM

TIME TO LEARN
11 MONTHS/1,100 HOURS

HINDI	341 million speakers
RUSSIAN	154 million speakers
TURKISH	80 million speakers
VIETNAMESE	76 million speakers

HARD

TIME TO LEARN
20 MONTHS/2,000 HOURS

CHINESE	1.3 billion speakers
ARABIC	319 million speakers
JAPANESE	128 million speakers
KOREAN	77 million speakers

CITY OF GOLD

Will left school at 14 and aside from getting married at 18 to a local farmer's daughter, Anne Hathaway, no one knows what he did next. Called the "lost years," some think he went to work for his dad, who'd gotten into debt. Others think he worked as a butcher or became an actor. Either way, sometime in the 1580s he said goodbye to his wife and kids and set off to find his fortune in the city of London.

BIG CITY

When Will moved to London it was one of the largest cities in Northern Europe, ten times the size of any other English town. England was quite an empty country—apart from all the sheep!

LONDON POPULATION:

1580s
200,000

Today
9 MILLION

St. Paul's Cathedral

River Thames

Bear Garden

The Swan

The Globe

The Rose

The Tower

KEY

 THEATER

QUEEN ELIZABETH I

When Will arrived in London, Elizabeth I was queen of England's Golden Age. A time of renaissance, she poured money into London's art scene and the city's first theaters were built.

THE GLOBE

Every week, thousands rowed across the Thames to visit the new open-air playhouses like the Swan, Rose, and Globe outside the city at Bankside.

BEAR GARDEN

Bear-baiting was a popular Tudor pastime. Huge dogs were let loose on a large bear that was chained to a stake in the middle of an arena, and the audience would gamble on the outcome. Queen Elizabeth was a big fan and in 1591 London theaters were banned from performing on Thursdays because that was the day bear-baiting took place!

The young Princess Elizabeth was one of the Tower of London's most famous inmates and her mom, Anne Boleyn, was beheaded there.

Today the Tower houses around:
23,500 JEWELS with a value of more than **$25 BILLION!**

People often used the river to get around because the streets were so crowded, which meant the Thames was full of small passenger boats called wherries.

ST. PAUL'S CATHEDRAL

Religion caused a lot of problems in Tudor times. Elizabeth was a Protestant, but she also had to deal with Catholics and Puritans.

RICH & POOR

As the city grew, poverty became a problem. The poor lived in **FILTHY, CROWDED** neighborhoods where **CRIME** was rife and **RAW SEWAGE** ran through the streets.

Average life expectancy was around:
35 YEARS

Most people living in cities didn't drink water. Because it was often mixed with sewage, it made people sick. Instead, grown-ups and children drank a weak beer. The alcohol helped to kill germs!

MONEY

There was no paper money in Tudor England, just coins. One shilling (12 pence) would buy you:

1x

1 HORSE for a day

2 DINNERS at an inn

12 LOAVES of bread

3 DOZEN eggs

4 SMALL pipes of tobacco

SHOWTIME!

In 1599, Will's acting company, the Lord Chamberlain's Men, built an open-air theater shaped like a donut and called it the Globe. Clever Will bought shares in it and staged his plays there. The more popular the theater became, the richer he grew!

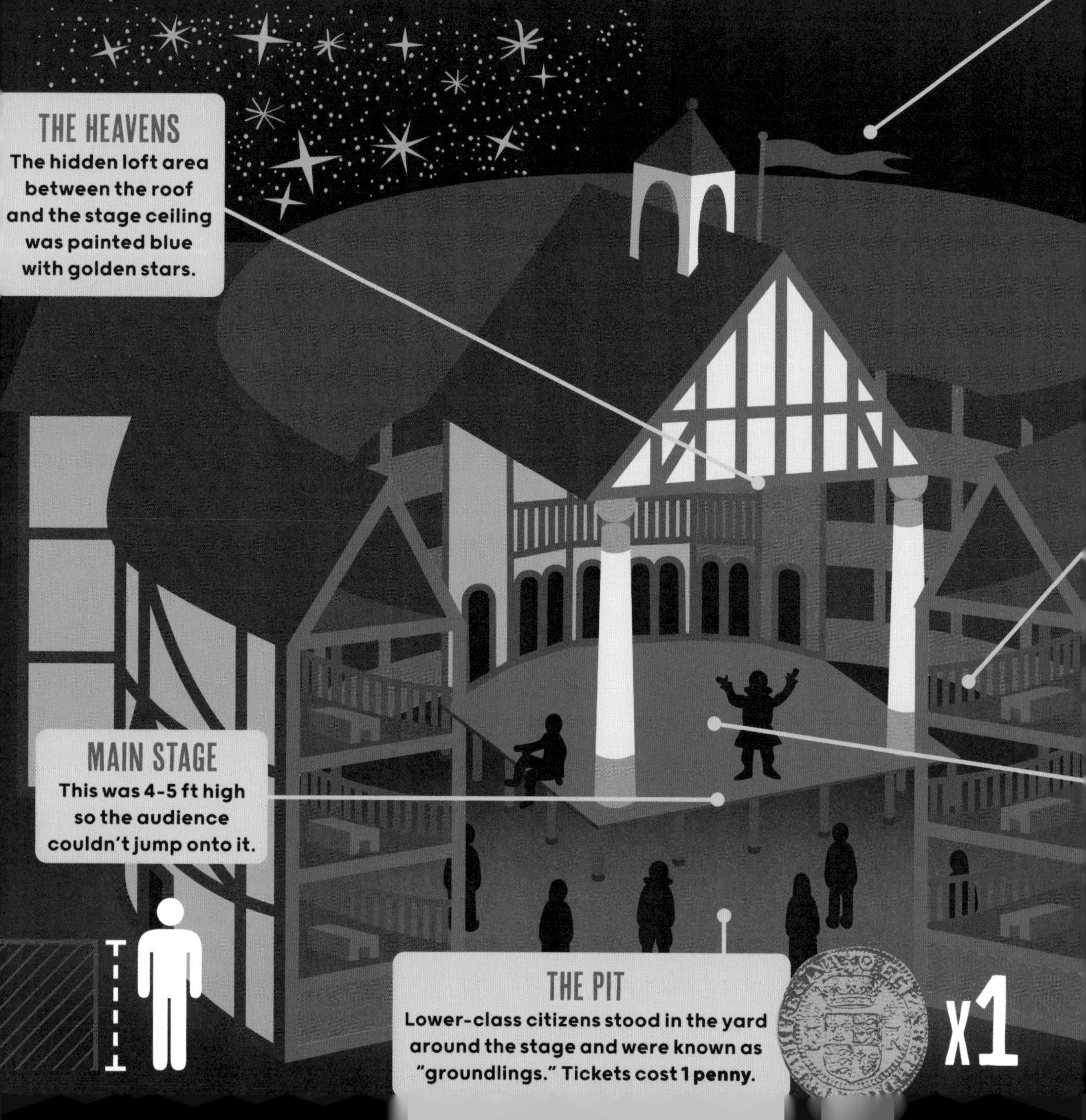

THE HEAVENS
The hidden loft area between the roof and the stage ceiling was painted blue with golden stars.
MAIN STAGE
This was 4-5 ft high so the audience couldn't jump onto it.
THE PIT
Lower-class citizens stood in the yard around the stage and were known as "groundlings." Tickets cost 1 penny.
X1

These were color-coded to show the kind of play being put on that day.

TRAGEDY

COMEDY

HISTORY

GALLERIES
Undercover seats were the most expensive at 2-6 pence each.

 x6

HELL
Actors playing ghosts or witches rose from the area beneath the stage through a trap door.

PLAYING FIRE

Acting companies in Will's time produced some dramatic special effects...

THUNDER
A cannonball rolled across the Heavens.

BIRD SONG
Bubbles blown in water.

LIGHTNING FLASH
A resin powder thrown into a candle flame.

LIGHTNING BOLTS
A firecracker attached to a wire between the roof and stage floor. Once lit, it shot from the top of the wire to the bottom, making sparks all the way!

FOG & FILTHY AIR
Saltpeter (made from dung) set alight.

BREATHING FIRE
A firecracker held in the actor's mouth!

GOOD SPIRITS
Came "flying in" on a wire through a trapdoor in the Heavens.

EVIL SPIRITS
Came up from Hell, out of a trapdoor in the stage.

BLOOD AND GORE
Packets made from animal bladders and filled with animal blood were hidden on the actor and split at the right moment.

10,000 VISITORS A WEEK

3,000 MAXIMUM CAPACITY

NO RESTROOMS!
People passed around a **BUCKET**

Actors learned **800** WORDS A DAY

MAKING FACES!

Women weren't allowed to act in Will's time because it was too unladylike, so boys dressed up as girls to play the female roles. The makeup they used was made from all kinds of weird (and poisonous!) ingredients...

PERFECTLY PALE SKIN

DEADLY

 + +

One cup of white lead powder + One spoon of water + Two spoons of vinegar

POISON-FREE VERSION:

 +

One cup of powdered hog bones + Four spoons of poppy oil

LUSCIOUS LIP AND CHEEK ROUGE

One cup of cochineal (tiny red insect) + Whites of two hard-boiled eggs + Two spoons of green fig milk + One spoon of acacia tree sap

LIGHTENING YELLOW HAIR DYE

DEADLY

 + + +

A quarter cup of saffron

A quarter cup of cumin seed

A quarter cup of celandine

Four spoons of oil

POISON-FREE VERSIONS:

Urine

Wear a wig!

GENDER SWAPS

In lots of his comedies Will makes things even more confusing by having female characters disguise themselves as men!

PIMPLE-FIGHTING FACIAL PEEL

 + + +

Whites of two eggs

One spoon of rose water

Half a spoon of plantain weed juice

Half a spoon of dock leaf juice

SHIMMERY SKIN HIGHLIGHTS

 +

Half a cup of crushed pearls

Half a cup of crushed silver

RUFFING IT

Large collars called ruffs were the height of fashion in Will's time. The biggest ones used up to six yards of material folded into 600+ pleats!

ELEMENTS OF SHAKESPEARE

Most of the plays that Will wrote can be split into three different types: tragedies, comedies, and histories. His tragedies are sad and there's lots of death, the comedies usually have happy (silly) endings, and the histories are based on past kings of England. Here are some of the other features he liked to put into his plays.

Sn

Supernatural

Witches, fairies, ghosts, floating daggers, and apparitions.

 A Midsummer Night's Dream, The Tempest
 Hamlet, Julius Caesar, Macbet

Tf
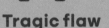
Tragic flaw

The hero has a character flaw (such as jealousy, ambition, or pride) that leads to their downfall.

 Hamlet, King Lear, Macbeth, Othello, Romeo & Juliet

R
Revenge

The hero has suffered a great wrong and wants revenge.

 Hamlet, Titus Andronicus

S

Soliloquy

A character talks to himself and reveals his thoughts.

 A Midsummer Night's Dream
 Hamlet, Macbeth, King Lear

C
Conflict

Family quarrels, rivals in love and war, difficult choices, good versus evil.

 King Lear, Macbeth, Romeo & Juliet

Fn

Fall of nobleman

A wealthy man of noble character loses everything.

 Hamlet, Julius Caesar, King Lear, Macbeth, Othello

M
Melancholy

Extreme stress causes mental health problems.

 Hamlet, King Lear, Macbeth

TRAGEDY

F
Fool

A clever servant or peasant points out the truth.

 As You Like It, Twelfth Night
King Lear

W
Wedding

The play ends with a marriage celebration.

As You Like It, The Merchant of Venice, The Tempest, Twelfth Night

Cd
Cross-dressing

Girl characters dress up as boys and boys as girls.

As You Like It, The Merchant of Venice, Twelfth Night

Ff
Fate and fortune

Characters can't change their destiny, however much they try.

The Merchant of Venice
Antony & Cleopatra, King Lear, Othello

L
Love

Lovers are separated and then reunited.

Love's Labour's Lost, Much Ado About Nothing

Mi
Mistaken identities

Characters disguise themselves or are mistaken for someone else.

As You Like It, The Comedy of Errors, Twelfth Night

P
Puns

Playing with words for dramatic effect.

 Hamlet, Romeo & Juliet
 Richard III

 ***#$!**

Ci
Colorful insults

Creative and hilarious put-downs.

 All's Well That Ends Well, Taming of the Shrew
 Henry IV, Part I

KEY TO PLAYS

 COMEDY

 TRAGEDY

 HISTORY

COMEDY

WORD PLAY

Will was a master at writing. With nail-biting plots full of everything from witches and fairies to revenge and obsession, his plays are more entertaining than you'd think. The language can be tricky to understand (it's 400 years old, after all) but once you see one of his plays, either on stage or screen, and begin to tune into the story, you realize how clever he was with language, especially when it came to insults!

HOW TO TALK LIKE Shakespeare

"Instead of **WHY**, say **WHEREFORE**.
Add "**ETH**" to the end of all verbs:
HE SWIMMETH, HE DIVETH, HE DROWNETH.
Instead of **YOU**, say **THOU.**
Call your friends "**COUSIN.**"
Instead of **HERE**, say **HITHER.**
Add **METHINKS** to the start of every sentence,
and **MERRILY** to the end.
IT IS becomes **TIS** and **IT WAS** becomes **TWAS.**
Instead of **LISTEN**, say **HARK.**"

INSULT GENERATOR

Create your own Shakesperean put-down and slay your enemies! Take one word from each of the columns on the right and add "Thou" to the start.

THOU →

1	2	3
beslubbering	bat-fowling	bum-bailey
dankish	beetle-headed	foot-licker
gorbellied	clay-brained	horn-beast
lumpen	fat-kidneyed	hugger-mugger
mammering	fool-born	jointhead
peevish	flap-mouthed	maggot-pie
pribbling	onion-eyed	pathetical nit
reeky	sheep-biting	pignut
spleeny	swag-bellied	promise-breaker
yeasty	unchin-snouted	worm

BEAT IT!

Will used a special rhythm in his plays called **IAMBIC PENTAMETER.**

It means every line has ten beats and, just like a heartbeat, every second beat is a bit longer than the first: da-dum, da-dum, da-dum, da-dum, da-dum. This makes Shakespeare really easy to rap! Try picking some lines of verse from one of his plays and see how easily they fit to a beat.

THIS IS AN IAMB

de-DUM

THIS IS AN IAMBIC PENTAMETER

⌣ — ⌣ — ⌣ — ⌣ — ⌣ —

BUT, SOFT! / WHAT LIGHT / THROUGH YOND / ER WIND / OW BREAKS?

Catchy phrase

FROM "PUPPY-DOG"

TO "LADYBIRD"

WILL FIRST USED NEARLY 1,700 WORDS!

And he loved making up new phrases too. Here are a few that he made popular, can you match them to their meanings?

Break the ice	A hopeless task
Dead as a doornail	In a difficult situation
Fancy free	Start a conversation with someone new
Tower of strength	Jealousy
Cold comfort	Free to do what you like
In stitches	Someone who can be relied on for support
Fair play	Not much help
In a pickle	Very dead
Green-eyed monster	Laughing uncontrollably
Wild-goose chase	Honest and equal behavior

WHO said WHAT?

Can you work out who said what below, pop star **JUSTIN BIEBER** or **WILL SHAKESPEARE**?

1. Now I'm all alone and my joys turned to moping.
2. May you dance do a spin.
3. All that glisters is not gold.
4. We are such stuff as dreams are made on.
5. I'll pick up the pieces if you come undone.
6. Was I a fool to let you break down my walls?
7. Nothing will come of nothing.
8. If music be the food of love, play on.

DID THOU KNOWETH?

The **LONGEST WORD** in Shakespeare is honorificabilitudinitatibus. It means "very honorable" in Latin and was spoken by Costard the clown in *Love's Labour's Lost*.

HONORIFICABILITUDINITATIBUS

• WILL •   • JUSTIN •

The Black Death

Deadly and highly contagious, the bubonic plague was a terrible disease that ravaged England in 1348. Between then and 1665 there were several more outbreaks, and anyone living at that time was lucky to escape with their life!

Odd Cures

Doctors didn't know about germs and didn't understand how the plague spread. They tried lots of weird ways to cure the sick . . .

Giving victims moldy, 10-year-old treacle to drink.

Covering lumps with a paste made from human poop and flower roots.

Rubbing the belly of a live frog over the victim's body.

Bathing in urine.

Plucking a live chicken's butt and rubbing it over the lumps.

Symptoms

RASHES

VOMITING BLOOD

HEADACHE

FEVER

EGG-SIZED LUMPS CALLED BUBOES IN THE NECK, ARMPITS, AND GROIN

DIFFICULTY BREATHING

Death IN 3 DAYS

The disease was caused by bites from fleas carried on rats. But back then people blamed it on:

- "BAD" AIR
- THE STARS & PLANETS
- GOD BEING ANGRY

HOW DID THE PLAGUE AFFECT WILL?

In 1564, the year Will was born, Stratford LOST A SIXTH of its population.

Will may have lost his sisters, MARGARET and ANNE, and his brother, EDMUND.

THEATERS were CLOSED DOWN during outbreaks.

Will's SON HAMNET DIED in 1596 AGED JUST 11, possibly from plague.

R.I.P.
HAMNET SHAKESPEARE
D. 1596

Will created some of the best characters of all time. Powerful, funny, or magical, they all stand out. So which one are you?

START HERE

PICK A SIDE

EVIL

Chanting over a cauldron → You are one of the **THREE WITCHES**

What's your favorite pastime? → Scheming and plotting → After dark I like to . . . → Sleepwalk → You are **LADY MACBETH**. You're beautiful and powerful

You are **IAGO**. You're one of Will's most sinister supervillains

Creep about carrying out evil plans

BIT OF BOTH

Are you ambitious? → No more than most → What do you think of revenge?

Yes, I want to be the best!

You are **MALVOLIO**. You're a vain, pompous servant ← What? Of course not!

GOOD

Are you a natural leader? → Um, I dunno → You are **JULIET**. You're a naive young girl

You are **THE NURSE**. You're Juliet's friend → Is a donkey involved?

You bet

Which love is the best? → Young and passionate → Rude and racy → Self-love

Do you like magic? → Nope, it's mumbo jumbo → Death or disguise?

Ooh yes, I love it

You are **JULIUS CAESAR**. You're the ruler of Rome

You are **OBERON**. You're King of the Fairies

You are **HAMLET**. You're the Prince of Denmark

What kind? → Fortune-telling → Love potions → Ghosts

WHICH SHAKESPEARE CHARACTER ARE YOU?

It's a waste of time

I'm consumed by it

You are SHYLOCK. You're a Jewish moneylender

What's your favorite food?

Berries and fish → You are CALIBAN. You're the son of a witch-hag

Anything and everything! → You are SIR JOHN FALSTAFF. You're a disgraced knight

Which do you prefer?

A dark sense of humor → You are RICHARD III. You're a power-hungry duke

Floating daggers → You are MACBETH. You're a brave Scottish nobleman

Afraid so... → You are BOTTOM. You're a weaver who loves acting

You are CORDELIA. You're King Lear's beautiful young daughter

Family devotion

Cross-dressing

Wish you had a twin?

No twins for me, thanks → You are ROSALIND. You're the daughter of a duke

You betcha! → You are VIOLA. You're a young aristocratic woman

Blood and guts, please

Isn't Ancient Britain amazing?

I prefer Italy → You are OTHELLO. You're an African general

Couldn't agree more → You are KING LEAR. You're a vain old king

You are PROSPERO. You're a powerful magician

Sorcery

BOOM!

In 1603 Queen Elizabeth I died, bringing the Tudor dynasty to an end. Her Scottish cousin, James Stuart, was crowned king, but he upset the Catholics and it wasn't long before they started plotting against him . . .

EVERY YEAR ON NOVEMBER 5TH THE BRITISH PEOPLE:

- Gather around roaring bonfires.
- Set off fireworks.
- Burn dummies of Guy Fawkes.

They rented a cellar under the English Parliament and smuggled in **36 BARRELS OF GUNPOWDER** which they hid beneath some firewood.

Meanwhile
A BAND OF 13 ANGRY CATHOLICS, fed up with Protestants leading the country, plotted to kill the king.

GUY FAWKES
SHERIFF'S DEPT.

The Catholic Lord Monteagle received an **ANONYMOUS LETTER WARNING** him not to attend the opening of Parliament on **NOVEMBER 5TH.** He showed it to the king.

SOLDIERS SEARCHED PARLIAMENT. They found the hidden gunpowder and caught one of the plotters, Guy Fawkes, red-handed, ready to light the fuse!

PARLIAMENT

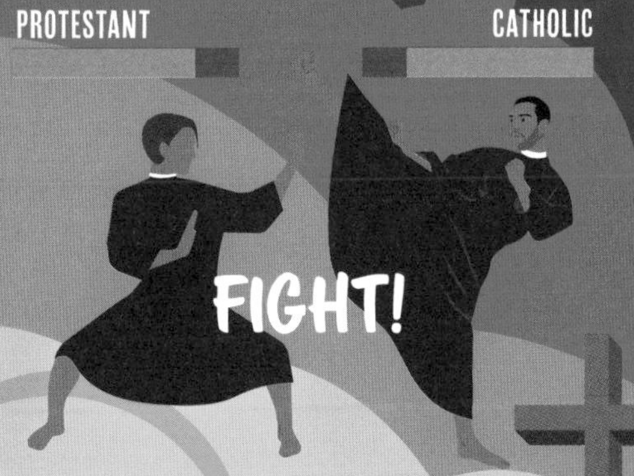
PROTESTANT
CATHOLIC
FIGHT!

"Remember, remember, the 5th of November,
Gunpowder treason and plot,
I see no reason why gunpowder treason
Should ever be forgot"

BONFIRE NIGHT HAS BEEN AROUND SINCE 1605, a time when the Catholics and Protestants were fighting (again).

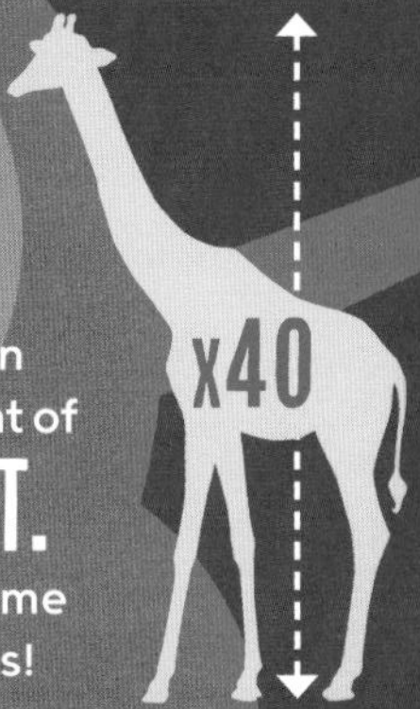
x40

Fireworks can reach a height of **655 FEET.** That's the same as 40 giraffes!

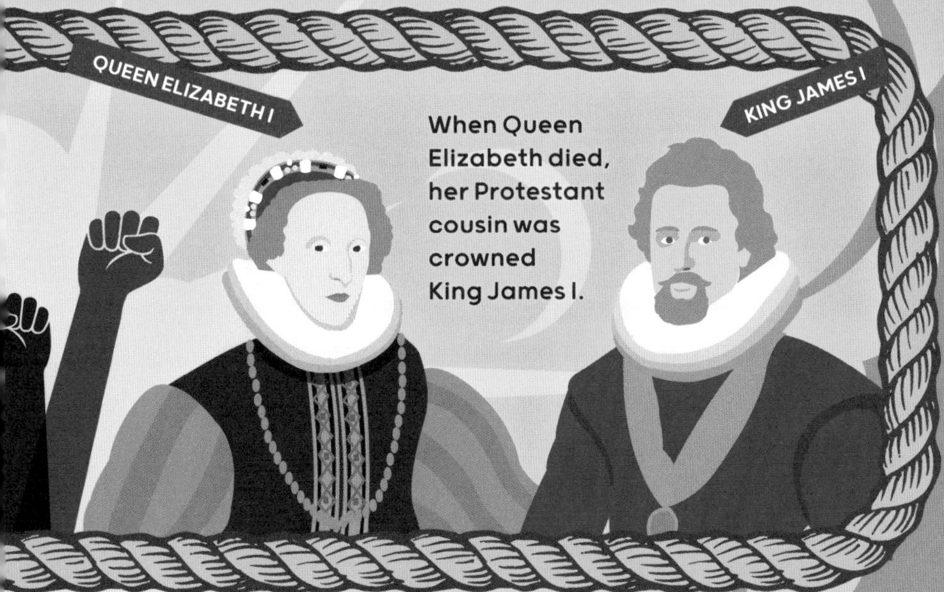
QUEEN ELIZABETH I
KING JAMES I

When Queen Elizabeth died, her Protestant cousin was crowned King James I.

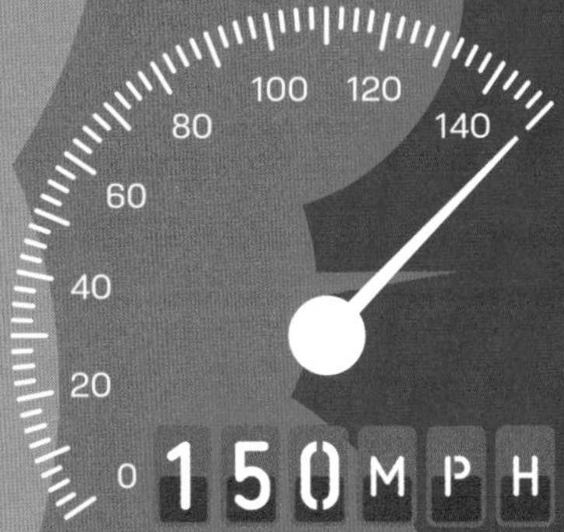
0
20
40
60
80
100
120
140
150 MPH

The speed a firework rocket can reach.

TAKEN TO THE TOWER OF LONDON, Guy soon gave up the names of his fellow conspirators and the king had them **HORRIBLY EXECUTED.** People celebrated with bonfires in the street and James declared **NOVEMBER 5TH A NATIONAL HOLIDAY.**

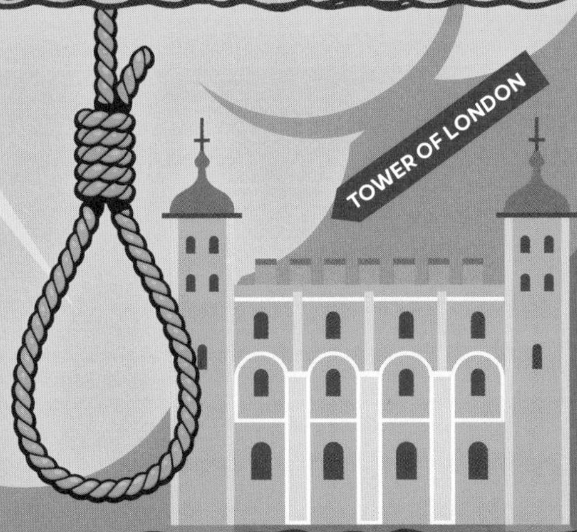
TOWER OF LONDON

DID YOU KNOW?

The Gunpowder Plot must have had a big impact on Will because his next play, MACBETH, was filled with references to it.

It's a play about:

TREASON

THE OVERTHROW OF A SCOTTISH KING

THE DOWNFALL OF HIS MURDERERS

DARK MAGIC

People in Will's time were incredibly superstitious. They blamed bad luck on witches, worried about evil spirits, and believed the stars and planets controlled their lives. Will took advantage of their fascination with the supernatural and used ghosts, fairies, and magic in lots of his plays to add spooky suspense . . .

WITCHES AT WORK

In Tudor times, when things went wrong, witches got the blame.

Crops not growing?
Has someone died?
An unexplained fire?
The death of an animal?
MUST BE A WITCH!

WITCHES

Most people believed in witches. King James I even wrote a guide to witch hunts! Will knew this and added witches to MACBETH to please him.

HOW TO **SPOT** A WITCH

SINGLE

OLD

♀

WOMAN

POOR

WHAT DID WITCHES DO?

People thought witches had made a pact with the Devil to gain magic powers. They could:

SEE INTO THE FUTURE

CREATE STORMS

CALL UP THE DEAD

CAUSE THE DEATH OF THEIR ENEMIES

SINK SHIPS

BECOME INVISIBLE

TRANSFORM INTO ANIMALS

3 WAYS
TO TEST FOR A WITCH

DUCKING

Throw her into a river with her hands and feet tied.

FLOATS? ▶ **A WITCH**

SINKS? ▶ **INNOCENT** (now probably drowned)

WITCH MARKS

Does she have a birthmark? That's been put there by the Devil!

FAMILIARS

Does she have a pet animal? It could be a demonic creature in disguise, ready to do her bidding!

RAT

RAVEN

CAT

TOAD

GHOSTS

Ghosts were accepted as perfectly real.

WILL INCLUDED 11 GHOSTS IN HIS PLAY RICHARD III

People believed they:
Were **RESTLESS SPIRITS** doomed to walk the Earth.

Emitted **STRANGE NOISES.**

Appeared to **PASS ON A MESSAGE** or **FINISH A TASK.**

BOO!

Queen Elizabeth's ghost is still said to haunt Windsor Castle!

There were some huge scientific discoveries in Will's time, but people struggled to separate them from superstition. The queen's astrologer, **DR. JOHN DEE**, is a perfect example of this. On the one hand he was a **GIFTED MATHEMATICIAN**, on the other he studied the **LANGUAGE OF ANGELS** and thought he could talk to them.

STARRY-EYED
Pretty much everyone believed in fate and astrology–the idea that their future was somehow "written in the stars." When a baby was born, women delivered it, while "doctors" studied the stars to work out how they'd affect the baby's life!

GOING FOR GOLD
Many respectable scientists tried to **TURN LEAD INTO GOLD** in a process called "alchemy."

EMPIRE OF THE SUN
Polish astronomer **NICOLAUS COPERNICUS** said that the Sun, not the Earth, was the center of our solar system. He was right, but not many people believed him!

HEAVENLY BODIES
In 1609, Italian scientist **GALILEO GALILEI** built a telescope and made some awesome discoveries. He saw:
- Thousands of stars, which no one had seen before.
- Craters and mountains on the moon's surface.
- Four moons orbiting Jupiter.

SUPERSTITION

GOOD LUCK

BAD LUCK

A COW'S BREATH

SPITTING IN A FIRE

TOUCHING A MAN WHO'S ABOUT TO DIE

SPILLING SALT

WALKING UNDER A LADDER

Beliefs in Will's time had a lot to do with good and evil. Some of them are still around today, others can seem a bit strange!

PEACOCK FEATHERS

SHOES ON A TABLE

BLACK CATS

BODY COUNT

In Will's tragedy plays, almost everyone dies. He kills off most of his characters by stabbing or poisoning them, because these were the easiest deaths to show in a theater. Trickier ones, like beheading, drowning, or baking people in pies (yum!), took place off stage.

No. of DEATHS

ROMEO & JULIET

Mercutio, Tybalt, and Paris
STABBED

Romeo
POISONS HIMSELF

Juliet
STABS HERSELF

Lady Montague
BROKEN HEART

HAMLET

Hamlet, Laertes, and Claudius
STABBED & POISONED

Gertrude
POISONED

Polonius
STABBED THROUGH A CURTAIN

Ophelia
DROWNED

Rosencrantz and Guildenstern
BEHEADED

MACBETH

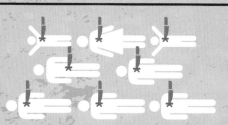

Duncan, Duncan's guards, Banquo, Lady Macduff and kids, and Young Siward
STABBED

Macbeth
BEHEADED

YAWN!

Lady Macbeth
EXHAUSTION

OTHELLO

Emilia and Roderigo
STABBED

Othello
STABS HIMSELF

Desdemona
SMOTHERED BY PILLOW

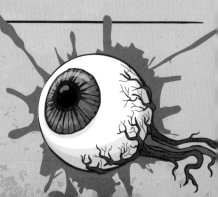

KING LEAR

IIII IIII
IIII IIII

Gloucester
BLINDED, HEART BURSTS

Edmund, Cornwall, and Oswald
STABBED

Goneril
STABS HERSELF

Regan
POISONED

Cordelia
HANGED

King Lear
BROKEN HEART

The Fool
VANISHES

ANTONY & CLEOPATRA

IIII

Enobarbus
GUILT

Antony
STABS HIMSELF

Iras
FALLS DOWN DEAD

Cleopatra and Charmian
SNAKEBITE

JULIUS CAESAR

IIII

Julius Caesar
STABBED

Brutus and Cassius
STAB THEMSELVES

Portia
SWALLOWS HOT COALS

Cinna the Poet
PULLED APART BY A MOB

TITUS ANDRONICUS

IIII IIII
IIII IIII
IIII

Alarbus
DISMEMBERED, BURNED

Chiron and Demetrius
STABBED AND BAKED INTO A PIE

Tamora
EATS SONS IN A PIE, STABBED

The Clown
HANGED

Titus
HAND CUT OFF, STABBED

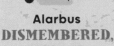 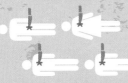

The Nurse, Mutius, Bassianus, and Saturninus
STABBED

Lavinia
HANDS CUT OFF, STABBED

Aaron
BURIED TO THE NECK, STARVED

Martius and Quintus
BEHEADED

CORIOLANUS   TIMON OF ATHENS   THE WINTER'S TALE

Coriolanus
TORN TO PIECES

Timon
DIES IN A CAVE

Antigonus
EATEN BY A BEAR

Last word!

Rich and famous, Will was so worried about GRAVE-ROBBERS digging up his bones that he put a CREEPY CURSE on his TOMBSTONE . . .

Will died on his birthday, **April 23, 1616** at the grand old age of **52**

GOOD FREND FOR IESVS SAKE FORBEARE,
TO DIGG THE DVST ENCLOASED HEARE.
BLESE BE Y͡E MAN Y͡T SPARES THES STONES,
AND CVRST BE HE Y͡T MOVES MY BONES.

The CURSE is still taken so seriously, in 2008 when builders needed to carry out repairs at HOLY TRINITY CHURCH in Stratford where WILL IS BURIED, they were careful not to DISTURB HIS BONES!

Death bed!

NOBODY KNOWS HOW WILL DIED. He made a will in the last few months of his life, which might mean he was ill and knew that he was dying. In it he mentions ANNE, HIS WIFE OF 34 YEARS, just once, right at the end, giving her one of his beds.

The "FURNITURE" was the COVERS FOR THE BED. To us this might seem mean, considering Will was so wealthy. But back then BEDS WERE VALUABLE HEIRLOOMS, used by people to show off their status, so ANNE MIGHT HAVE BEEN PLEASED!

"I GYVE UNTO MY WIEF MY SECOND BEST BED WITH THE FURNITURE."

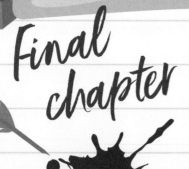

Final chapter

NONE OF WILL'S ORIGINAL SCRIPTS SURVIVE. Playwrights at the time often tried to keep their works out of print to stop them being copied by others. Seven years after Will died, two of his friends and fellow actors, John Heminges and Henry Condell, wrote out his plays, probably from copies of scripts, and published them under the name the First Folio. It's the only reason many of his plays are still around today!

Folio facts

36 plays

900 pages

Mr. WILLIAM SHAKESPEARES COMEDIES, HISTORIES, & TRAGEDIES

ONLY 750 PRINTED

PRICE £1

A copy of the First Folio recently sold at auction in New York for almost **$10 MILLION!**

THE WORD **LOVE** APPEARS **2,191** TIMES

233 COPIES survive today.

WILL WROTE AT LEAST:

37 plays

154 sonnets

Will's plays have been translated into more than **100 LANGUAGES,** including Esperanto, Interlingua, and *Star Trek*'s **KLINGON**

His plays have inspired at least **1,200 MOVIE AND TV ADAPTATIONS.** He's the most filmed author EVER!

Hamlet is the world's most widely performed play. They say it's being shown somewhere every minute of every day!

1x/MIN

Bonafide Bard?

CONFIDENTIAL

There's a **CONSPIRACY** that **WILL DIDN'T WRITE** his plays. Some scholars think the son of a glove-maker who never went to university couldn't possibly be the greatest writer of all time!

They've suggested at least **50 OTHER WRITERS** who might be the author, but all the **EVIDENCE** points to Will being the real deal.

CLASSIFIED

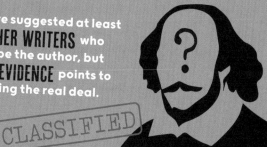

SECRET SCRIPTURE

In the KING JAMES BIBLE the 46TH WORD of PSALM 46 is "SHAKE" and the 46TH WORD from the end of the same Psalm is "SPEAR." Some people think this was a hidden birthday message to Will, as it was commissioned by his good friend KING JAMES I and written in 1610, the year of Will's 46TH BIRTHDAY!

There are **27** moons around Uranus and all but two are named for characters from Shakespeare.

GLOSSARY

Anonymous
When a person's name or identity is unknown.

Catholic
A member of the Catholic Church, the oldest branch of Christianity.

Conspirator
A person who plots secretly with others to do something bad or illegal.

Fate
When the events in someone's life are already decided.

First Folio
The first published collection of Shakespeare's plays.

Hornbook
A wooden tablet used to teach children the alphabet in Tudor times.

Iambic pentameter
A type of verse with ten beats per line.

Merchant
A person who buys and sells goods.

Petty School
A small Tudor school for children aged four to six.

Plague
A contagious disease that killed millions of people in medieval England.

Playhouse
A type of theater built in Elizabethan times.

Protestant
A branch of Christianity that began in "protest" against the Catholic Church.

Puritan
Very strict Protestants who wanted to lead simple lives and "purify" their religion.

Renaissance
A period of time in history when there were lots of exciting new ideas in science, art, and philosophy.

Ruff
A round, pleated collar worn in Elizabethan times.

Sonnet
A type of poem with 14 lines made popular by Shakespeare.

Superstition
A belief that isn't based on facts or reality.

Tanner
A person who makes leather from animal skins.

Treason
The crime of betraying your own country.

Tudor
The royal family that ruled England from 1485 to 1603.

First published 2021 by Button Books, an imprint of Guild of Master Craftsman Publications Ltd, Castle Place, 166 High Street, Lewes, East Sussex, BN7 1XU, UK. Copyright in the Work © GMC Publications Ltd, 2021. ISBN 978 1 78708 051 5. Distributed by Publishers Group West in the United States. All rights reserved. No part of this publication may be reproduced, stored in a retrieval system, or transmitted in any form or by any means without the prior permission of the publisher and copyright owner. While every effort has been made to obtain permission from the copyright holders for all material used in this book, the publishers will be pleased to hear from anyone who has not been appropriately acknowledged and to make the correction in future reprints. The publishers and authors can accept no legal responsibility for any consequences arising from the application of information, advice, or instructions given in this publication. A catalogue record for this book is available from the British Library. Senior Project Editor: Susie Duff. Design: Tim Lambert, Matt Carr. Illustrations: Alex Bailey, Matt Carr, Shutterstock. Color origination by GMC Reprographics. Printed and bound in China.

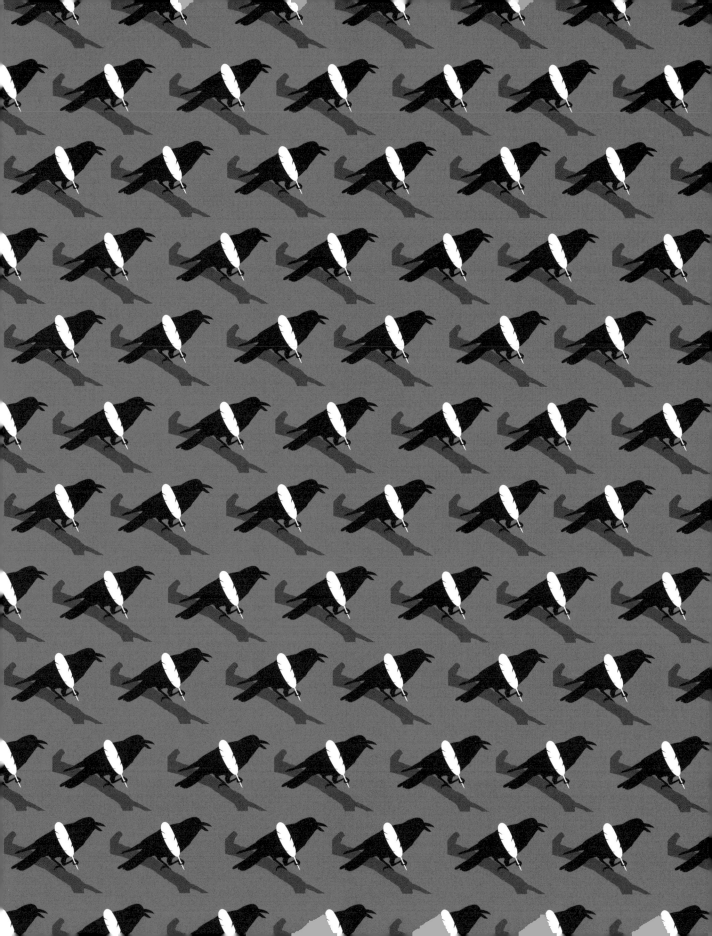

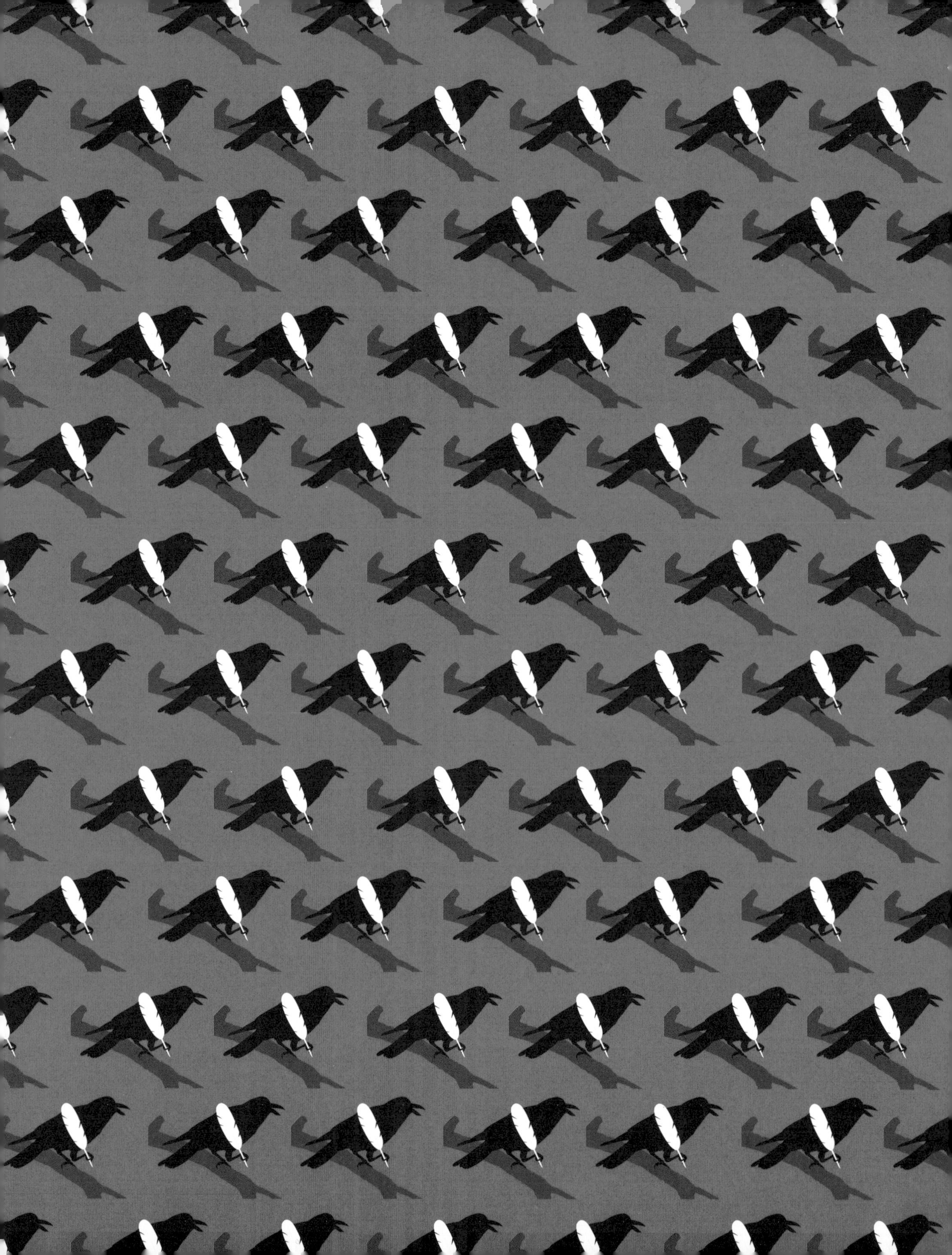